MY LITTLE GOLDEN BOOK ABOUT

K-POP

ULTIMATE FAN EDITION

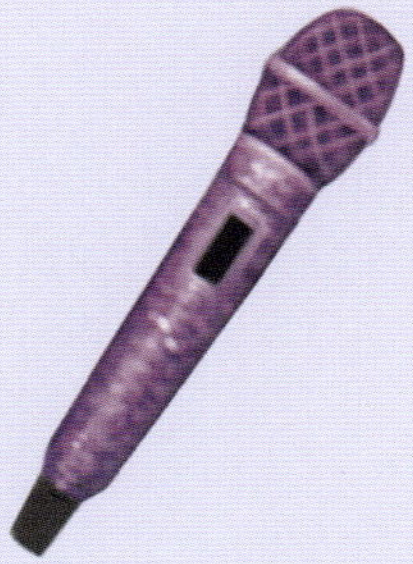

For Noah and Luna. I'm your ultimate fan! —J.Y.

For mom, my forever star —S.P.

Golden Books
An imprint of Random House Children's Books
A division of Penguin Random House LLC
1745 Broadway, New York, NY 10019
penguinrandomhouse.com
rhcbooks.com

Originally published in a slightly different form as *My Little Golden Book About K-pop* by Golden Books, an imprint of Random House Children's Books, a division of Penguin Random House LLC, New York, in 2026.
Library of Congress Cataloging-in-Publication Data is available upon request.
ISBN 979-8-217-23335-9 (trade)
Manufactured in China
10 9 8 7 6 5 4 3 2 1
EU Contact: Penguin Random House Ireland, 32 Nassau Street, Dublin D02 YH68.
https://eu-contact.penguin.ie

MY LITTLE GOLDEN BOOK ABOUT

K-POP

ULTIMATE FAN EDITION

By Jessica Yoon ✦ Illustrated by Suji Park

A GOLDEN BOOK • NEW YORK

Girls' Generation
BTS
BLACKPINK

K-pop is short for Korean popular music, a blend of pop, hip-hop, R&B, electronic music, and more! K-pop also features high-energy choreography and eye-catching visuals.

Modern K-pop began in the 1990s. Over time, its popularity spread to other countries in a phenomenon called Hallyu, or "the Korean wave." Today, there are millions of K-pop fans all over the world!

Seo Taiji and Boys are considered the first modern K-pop group. In 1992, they debuted the song "난 알아요 (I Know)" on a live televised talent show. Their performance included rap, rock, and breakdancing. The group received the lowest score of the night. But teen viewers loved them! Their song topped the music charts for weeks.

Seo Taiji and Boys paved the way for the first wave of K-pop. This included groups like H.O.T., Sechs Kies, S.E.S., Fin.K.L, g.o.d, and Shinhwa.

In 1996, H.O.T. released their iconic song “Candy.” The ski clothes they wore in the music video led to a fashion craze. Everyone wanted fluffy mittens!

S.E.S.

Shoo Bada (Sea) Eugene

Hyunjin (Stray Kids)

Yeji (ITZY)

S.E.S. was one of the first K-pop girl groups. Right before a new tour, they dyed their hair different colors. This change got them banned from South Korean TV shows. But it didn't stop fans from buying their albums! Now K-pop idols express themselves with all different hair colors.

j-hope (BTS)

Taeyong (NCT) Soobin (TXT) Dahyun (TWICE)

When South Korea faced hard times, the government realized K-pop's popularity could help the country. They supported entertainment companies that created the idol training system to find more K-pop stars. Trainees practiced singing and dancing, worked hard, and followed strict rules—all in the hopes of becoming famous. These training programs still exist today.

By the 2000s, second-generation K-pop groups, like TVXQ, Girls' Generation, BIGBANG, Wonder Girls, 2NE1, and SHINee, became famous throughout Asia. Solo artists like Rain and BoA—the Queen of K-pop—gained popularity, too. They began to release songs in different languages to reach more fans.

TVXQ and Girls' Generation were the first to include photo cards in their albums. Fans collected and traded these cards—something they still do today!

TVXQ was also the first group to create an official fandom name—Cassiopeia. Now all K-pop fandoms have their own names!

BIGBANG, known as the Kings of K-pop, started a new fad, too. In 2006, they introduced crown-shaped light sticks designed by G-Dragon, one of the group's members. Now custom light sticks are a huge part of every K-pop concert experience. Fans love waving their light sticks in unison to create a light show!

G-Dragon also started a trend where celebrities treat airports like fashion runways. He and other K-pop idols, like Hwasa from MAMAMOO and Hanni from NewJeans, use their travel outfits to give fans style inspiration!

In 2012, K-pop became even more popular with PSY's hit song "Gangnam Style." PSY's catchy song and dance moves became a pop culture phenomenon. The music video, which also features the K-pop star Hyuna, became the first YouTube video ever to reach one billion views!

In the 2010s, YouTube and social media helped propel the third generation of K-pop idols to global stardom. This included groups like BTS, BLACKPINK, EXO, TWICE, SEVENTEEN, and Red Velvet.

Third-generation groups focused on telling stories with their songs to connect with fans. They also made high-quality music videos that looked like scenes from movies!

Fan-favorite group BTS has won hundreds of awards and set many world records for song streams, video views, and album sales!

Its members sing about self-love, mental health, and following your dreams. They also promote these ideas off-stage, by working for social causes and sharing their positive messages with world leaders. Their fans, called ARMY, love their dynamite mix of singing, rapping, and dance moves.

During this time, entertainment companies looked for talent in other countries, too. For example, while BLACKPINK's members Jisoo and Jennie auditioned in Seoul, South Korea, Rosé was recruited from Australia and Lisa was recruited from Thailand.

Today, they light up the sky together as one of the world's most popular girl groups. Their fans—BLINKs—love their hit songs about being strong and confident girls. BLACKPINK was the first Asian headliner at the Coachella music festival in California!

The fourth generation of K-pop started in 2018. It included groups like Stray Kids, aespa, ITZY, TOMORROW X TOGETHER, and ENHYPEN. Idols from this generation were especially good at using social media. They would sometimes gain international fans before they even debuted!

The group Stray Kids was formed on a Korean reality show. They have broken several records with their chart-topping albums!

STRAY KIDS

The year 2023 marked the start of fifth-generation groups. This includes ZEROBASEONE, RIIZE, BOYNEXTDOOR, BABYMONSTER, and KATSEYE. Some of these groups were formed on reality competitions.

KATSEYE's show aired on YouTube. With members from three continents, they are considered the first global girl group!

The group BABYMONSTER was supposed to debut with only five members. But fans loved all seven trainees so much, the entertainment company decided to debut them all!

K-pop is so popular that even animated idols can break records! In 2025, Sony Entertainment released the film *KPop Demon Hunters*. The movie included characters from Korean folklore, like the beloved tiger and magpie, and of course everything K-pop!

The movie's K-pop groups, HUNTR/X and Saja Boys, both hit the *Billboard* charts with songs like "Golden" and "Soda Pop." Three TWICE members—Jeongyeon, Jihyo, and Chaeyoung—recorded a version of the song "Takedown" just for the movie!

The award-winning film became Netflix's most-viewed movie ever, creating a whole new generation of K-pop fans!

The popularity of K-pop shows how music has the power to bring people together across languages and cultures. It is also a way to learn about Korean people and their history, and to make the world a more inclusive place. In the future, K-pop will continue to push boundaries, always evolving for the fans!

K-POP

The Global Sensation!

K-pop is full of incredible songs and performances. Whether you're a fan of pop, hip-hop, R&B, electronic music, rock, or another genre, K-pop has something for you!

Beyond the music, K-pop is rich with history and culture. Turn the page to learn more about the place where it all began.

The Home of K-pop: South Korea!

Official name: Republic of Korea
Capital: Seoul
Language: Korean
Population: 51.1 million people

Did You Know?

- South Korea is located on the continent of Asia.
- Seventy percent of the country is mountainous.
- South Korea is a peninsula, which is land surrounded by water on three sides.
- The national animal is the Siberian tiger.
- The national martial art is Taekwondo.
- The most popular sports are baseball and football (soccer).
- Two of the biggest holidays in South Korea are Seollal (Lunar New Year) and Chuseok (a harvest festival).

CHINA
NORTH KOREA
East Sea
Seoul
Incheon
SOUTH KOREA
Yellow Sea
Daegu
Busan
Jeju-do

Haute Hanbok

K-pop idols are stylish trendsetters who combine history and fashion. Some stars have worn outfits based on traditional Korean clothing called hanbok.

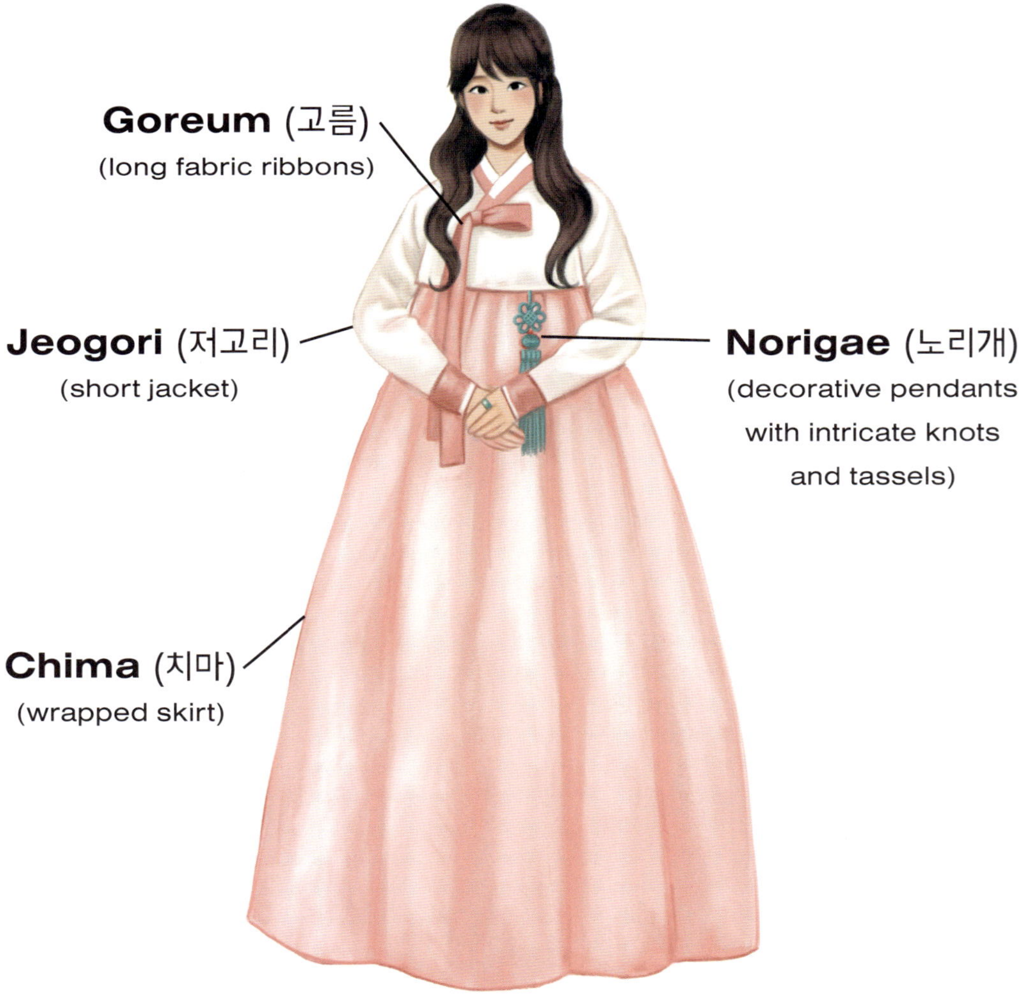

Jisoo (BLACKPINK)

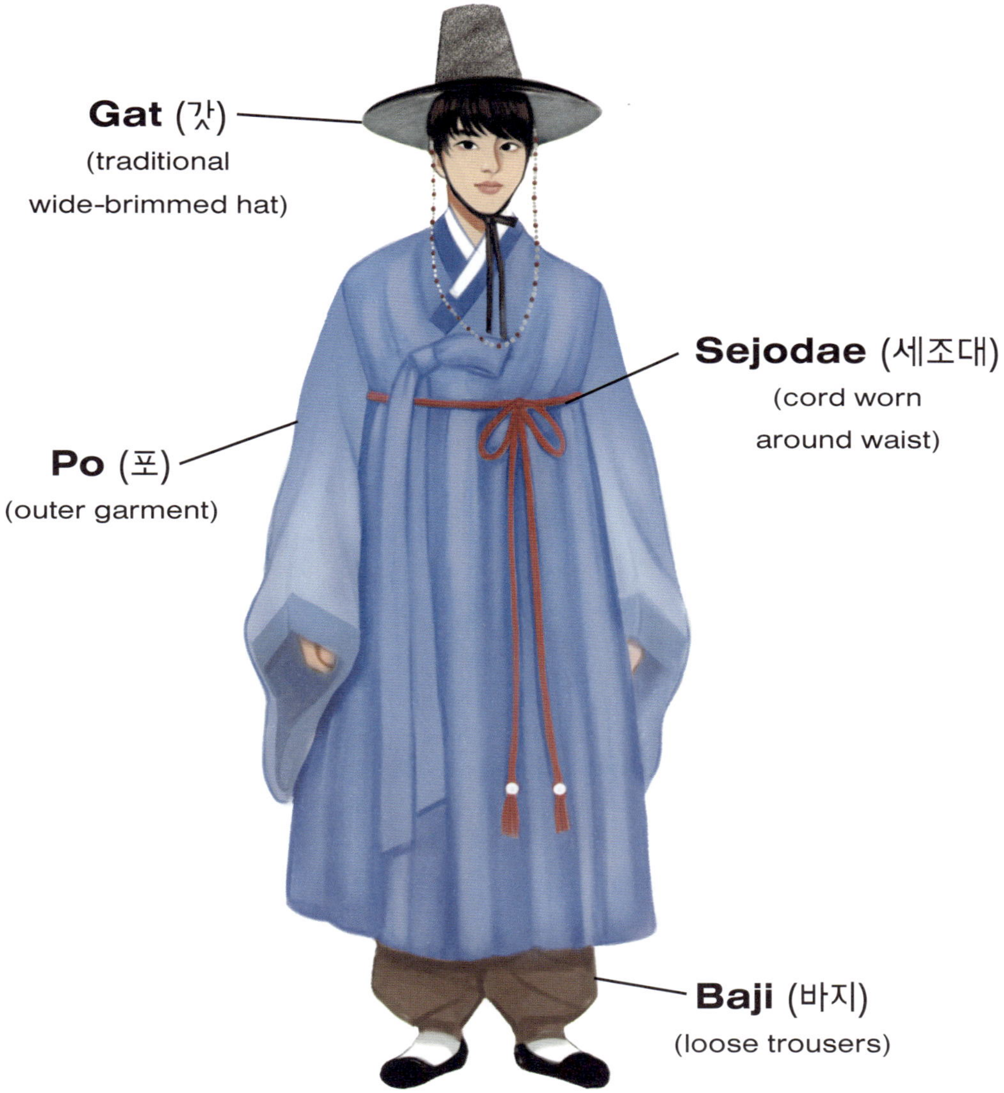

Jin (BTS)

Fun Fact: Hanbok is worn on special occasions like weddings, birthdays, and holidays such as Lunar New Year.

Light the Way!

Light sticks make K-pop concerts extra exciting! Each group has a unique light stick design their fans use at concerts.

If you were a K-pop star, what would your light stick look like?

Draw it here!

Who's Who?

Did you know that K-pop has its own vocabulary? Here are some popular terms and what they mean.

Group roles: Each member focuses on vocals, rapping, or dancing. Within each of these skills, members are assigned a role.

- **Main**: The member with the highest skill level
- **Lead**: The member with the second highest skill level
- **Sub**: A supporting act

Bias: Your favorite member of the group

Who's your bias in your favorite group?

Write it here: ______________________________

Bias wrecker: The group member who could make you switch biases

Who's your bias wrecker?

Write it here: ______________________________

Subunit: A smaller group within an idol group

Fun Fact: Subunits can be based on friend groups, languages members speak, or other reasons.

Solo stan: A fan who only cares about one member of the group

Maknae (막내): The youngest member of a group

Sunbae (선배): Senior, or the title a K-pop idol would use for another idol who debuted earlier than them

Hoobae (후배): Junior, or the title a K-pop idol would use for another idol who debuted after them

Name Game

Just like their fans, many K-pop idols have fun nicknames. Write the words below backward on the lines to find out the nicknames of each star!

Jimin (BTS): IHCOM

Jin (BTS): EMOSDNAH EDIWDLROW

Jisoo (BLACKPINK): TIBBAR ELTRUT

Fun Fact: This is a middle name she created for herself because she didn't have one!

I.N (Stray Kids): DAERB YBAB

____

Felix (Stray Kids): ENIHSNUS

____

Dahyun (TWICE): UBUD

____

Fun Fact: This word means “tofu” in Korean!

What would your nickname be if you were a K-pop star?

Hint: Think about some of your favorite things for inspiration!

Write it here: ______________________________

Have You Eaten?

K-pop idols love their favorite Korean foods.
Want to enjoy some of these delicious snacks?
Circle the ones you've tried or want to try.

Gimbap (김밥)

Eomuk (어묵)

Tteokbokki (떡볶이)

Dalgona (달고나)

Honeycomb toffee candy

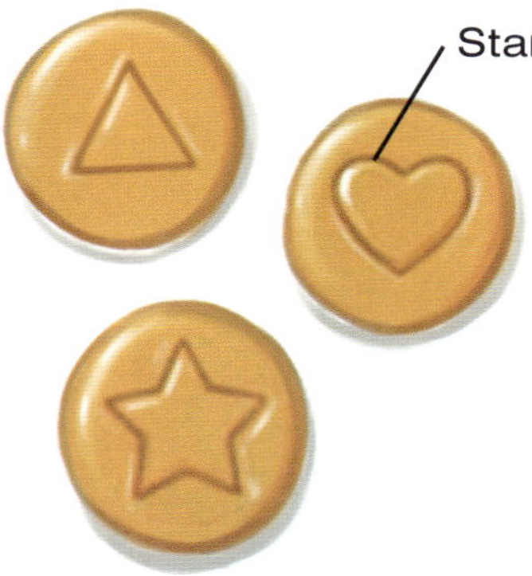

Hotteok (호떡)

Korean Corn Dog

Fun Fact: Some Korean corn dogs have French fries in the coating!

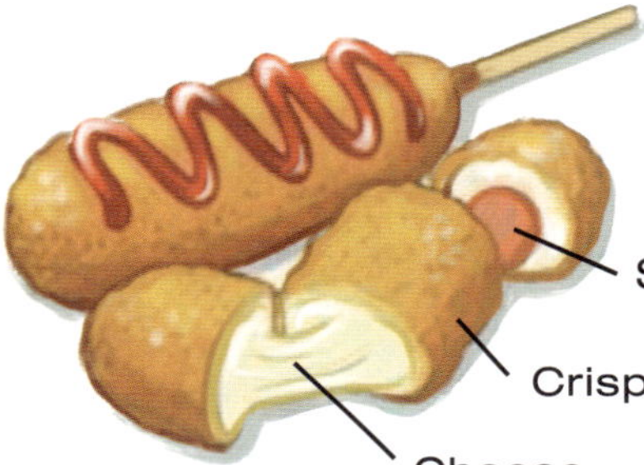

Ramyeon (라면)

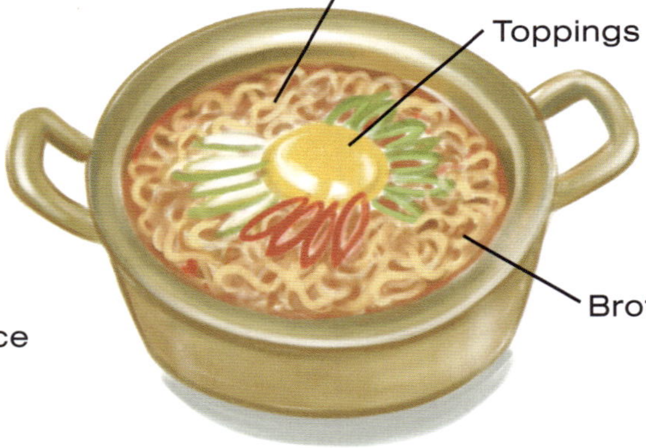

Bingsu (빙수)

Kimchi (김치)

Did You Know?

There are hundreds of different types of kimchi! It can be made with cabbage, radish, cucumbers, scallion, and much more. It's usually spicy, but there are non-spicy versions, too.

Fab Collab

Throughout the years, K-pop idols have worked with artists from around the world to make incredible music. Here are a few of their amazing collaborations!

BTS ft. Halsey – “Boy With Luv”

BTS: Halsey, Coldplay, Megan Thee Stallion, Steve Aoki

Jung Kook: Usher

TOMORROW X TOGETHER: Anitta

G-Dragon of BIGBANG: Anderson .Paak

Rosé and Bruno Mars – "APT."

BLACKPINK: Dua Lipa, Selena Gomez, Lady Gaga, Cardi B

Rosé: Bruno Mars

Lisa: Doja Cat and RAYE, Maroon 5, Rosalía

TWICE: Megan Thee Stallion

Wendy of Red Velvet: John Legend

Changbin: F.HERO and Milli

Who do you want to see collaborate?

Write it here: ____

Fan Favorites

Each K-pop act has their own group of fans with a special name. Can you match each group below with their fandom?

1 BTS
2 BLACKPINK
3 Stray Kids
4 TWICE
5 SEVENTEEN
6 EXO
7 BIGBANG
8 NCT
9 TOMORROW X TOGETHER
10 HUNTR/X
11 Saja Boys

A CARAT
B ONCE
C MOA
D NCTzen
E EXO-L
F ARMY
G Hunters
H BLINK
I The Pride
J V.I.P
K STAY

What are your favorite fandoms?

List them here:

________________ ________________

________________ ________________

Answer key: 1F; 2H; 3K; 4B; 5A; 6E; 7J; 8D; 9C; 10G; 11I

Stars of the Screen

Did you know many K-pop idols are also actors?

Rain made it on the Hollywood big screen with movies like *Speed Racer*.

Lisa from **BLACKPINK** acted in the third season of *The White Lotus*.

The group **Red Velvet** voiced the K-pop Gang in *Trolls World Tour!*

The artist **IU** has starred in many K-drama series, like *When Life Gives You Tangerines*.

Yoona from **Girls' Generation** starred in K-dramas like *Bon Appétit, Your Majesty*.

Star Power

K-pop idols support causes that are important to them.

- **IU** is well-known for her philanthropy. She has supported low-income families, disability awareness, and more!
- **BTS** spoke out against anti-Asian hate crimes in the United States. Along with their record label, they also donated one million dollars to Black Lives Matter.

- Many K-pop stars work as UNICEF ambassadors to help children around the world. **BTS** and **TOMORROW X TOGETHER** launched UNICEF campaigns to help children worldwide and improve mental health.

- **BLACKPINK** were climate ambassadors for the United Nations. They used their fame to encourage people to protect the environment.

You Be the Star!

In addition to performing, many K-pop idols write their own lyrics! Now it's time for you to express yourself. Write your own song lyrics below!

Speak Up!

"When things get tough, look at the people who love you! You will get energy from them."
—j-hope (BTS)

"I am happy to be in an era where people are open to new culture, new music. Who would imagine at Coachella thousands of people singing in Korean?"
—Jennie (BLACKPINK)

"No matter who you are, where you're from, your skin color, your gender identity: just speak yourself."
—RM (BTS)

K-pop Vibes

K-pop is so much more than just music. It includes people, history, culture, fashion, friendship, and of course, the fans! What does K-pop mean to you? Write it below!